David Paul Werner
Chi Ying Lam

Luna's Little Organ Book

Twenty-six pieces for one manual

Table of Contents

2:00 a.m. 2

Lost Star...3

Teddy's Day 4

Phrygigian..6

Prayer 7

Caprice on "Ton-y-Botel" 8

Reverie..9

Challenge Jig 10

Preludes on "Aberystwyth"..12

Four Hymn-settings:

    "Regent Square" 14

    "Helft mir Gotts Güte preisen" 14

    "Patmos"...15

    "St. Cross"..16

Bicinium: Passion Chorale 16

Three Settings on "Gelobt sei Gott".....................................18

Toccata Sognai...20

Three Settings on "Coronation"...21

Adagietto..23

Addendum: Setting on "Noël Nouvelet" 24

The pieces herein have been adapted to be playable on one manual without pedal. Original versions may be found in the publications below. Some of the original versions are longer or extracted from a longer work.

Publication	Title	for
The Trees Shall Sing!	"Coronation"	1 Man., Ped.
	"Gelobt sei Gott"	1 Man., Ped.
	"Helft mir Gotts Güte preisen"	1 Man., Ped.
	"Noël Nouvelet"	1 or 2 Man., opt. Ped.
	"Patmos"	1 Man., Ped.
	"Regent Square"	1 or 2 Man., opt. Ped.
	"St. Cross"	1 Man., Ped.
Eleven Chorale Settings for Organ	Bicinium: Passion Chorale	2 Man.
	Caprice on "Ton-y-Botel"	1 Man.
	Prayer	2 Man., Ped.
	Preludes on "Aberystwyth"	2 Man., Ped.
Eleven Diverse Pieces for Organ	Adagietto, from Toccata Concertino	2 Man.
	Challenge Jig	1 or 2 Man.
	Reverie	1 or 2 Man., opt. Ped.
	Toccata Sognai	1 or 2 Man., opt. Ped.

Performance notes

This collection consists of twenty-six pieces playable on a single manual having a minimum compass of 54-notes, C to f″′.

While the pieces are effective with a single stop, general registration suggestions tend to outline a cornet ensemble typical of smaller organs, *i.e.*, 8′, 4′, $2^2/_3$′, 2′, $1^3/_5$′. The Quint ($2^2/_3$′ or $1^1/_3$′) would be used in place of a mixture, the Tierce ($1^3/_5$′ or Sesquialtera) in place of a reed. The pieces can, of course, be registered more elaborately according to available resources.

Included are eleven hymn settings, on "Coronation", "Gelobt sei Gott", "Helft mir Gotts Güte preisen", "Noël Nouvelet", "Patmos", "Regent Square" and "St. Cross". These settings are suitable to accompany congregational singing. With adjustments to tempo and registration, they can serve also as preludes, offertories, postludes, *etc.*

Careful attention must be paid to notation of accidentals. Several pieces contain diminished and augmented unisons and octaves. Rather than indicate cautionary accidentals, it is left to the performer to assiduously apply this standard practice:

- An accidental pertains to a particular polyphonic voice at a particular vertical position on the staff. (It does not apply to other octaves, other staves or other polyphonic voices on the staff.) An accidental is canceled at the subsequent barline or, if the inflected note is tied across a barline, at the end of its duration.

D. P. W.

2:00 a.m.

Chi Ying Lam
Soft 8' 4' with Quintadena or Nazard, opt. Trem.
Relaxed
tenuous
a tempo
slowing to end
*At m. 11, on manuals with compass to f''', play f#'''' one
octave lower than written. Play grace note e'''' as written.

Lost Star

Chi Ying Lam

Teddy's Day
Adventure Suite

Chi Ying Lam

1. Teddy does Homework

2. Teddy Dancing

3. Hunter Chasing Teddy
+8', Quint
urgent
slower

4. Teddy Exhausted and Home in Time for Dinner
Bourdon 8' solo
slower
Phrygigian
Chi Ying Lam
=100~138
Recorder or Regal

Prayer

David Paul Werner

Caprice on "Ton-y-Botel"

David Paul Werner

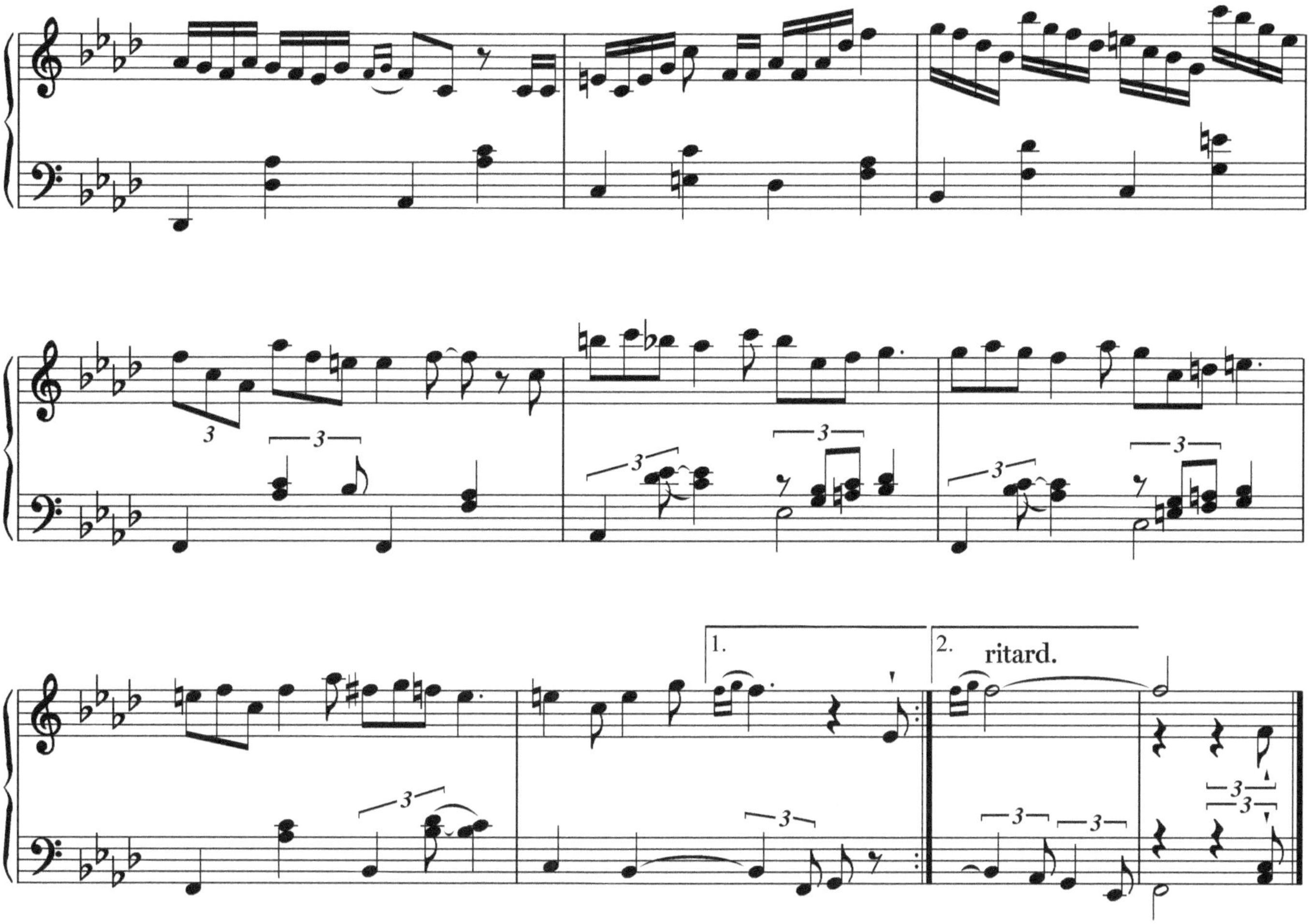

Reverie

on a chant donné

David Paul Werner

Largo sostenuto ♪=69~76

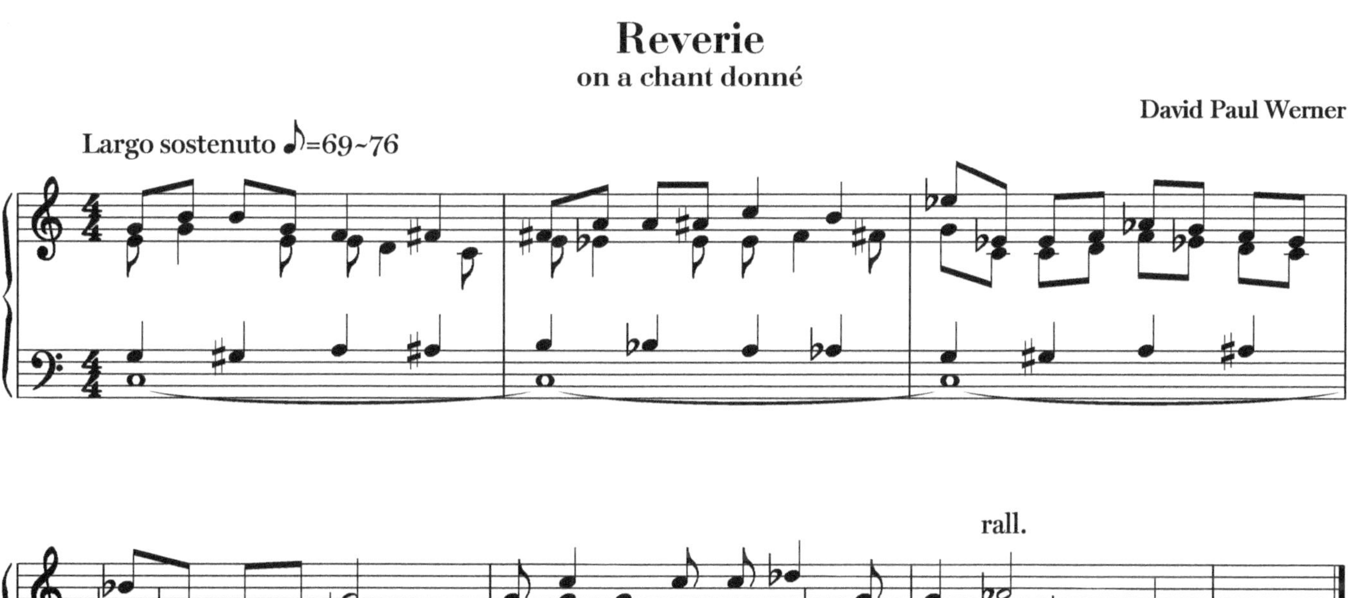

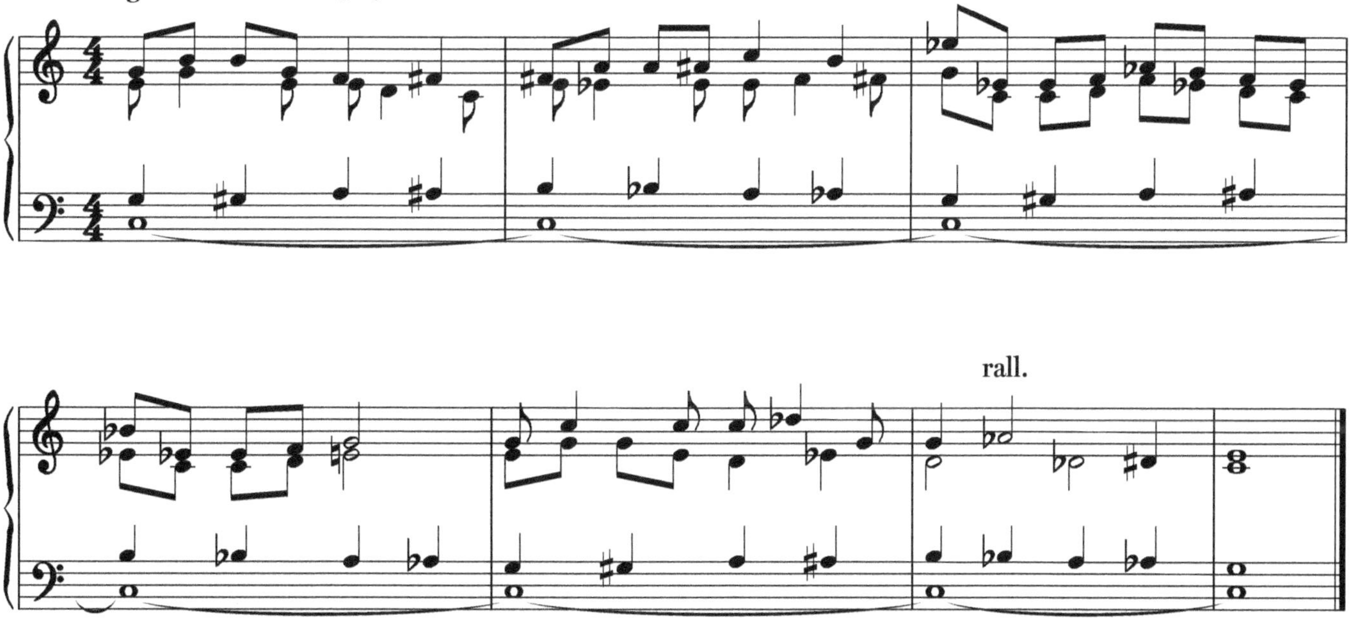

Challenge Jig

David Paul Werner

riten.   a tempo
(no rit.)
D.S. %
tempo giusto fino alla fine
CODA

Prelude on "Aberystwyth"

David Paul Werner

Alternate version, tune explicit

Four Hymn-settings

David Paul Werner

Regent Square

Patmos

St. Cross

Bicinium: Passion Chorale

A crown of thorns they put on his head, and a reed in his right hand.
They mocked him, saying, "Hail, king of the Jews!"   They spat
on him, and they took the reed and struck him on the head.

David Paul Werner

tr
1.
2.
8
arabesco libero
7
tr
rallen. poco a poco fino alla fine

Three Settings on "Gelobt sei Gott"

David Paul Werner

+ Mixture, Reed

Toccata Sognai

Three Settings on "Coronation"

David Paul Werner

più legato
marcato
— 22 —

Adagietto
from "Toccata Concertino"

David Paul Werner

Addendum: Setting on "Noël Nouvelet"

David Paul Werner

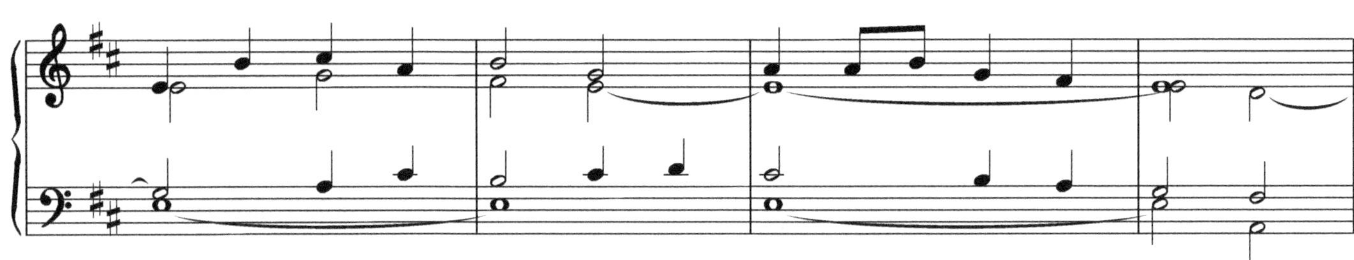

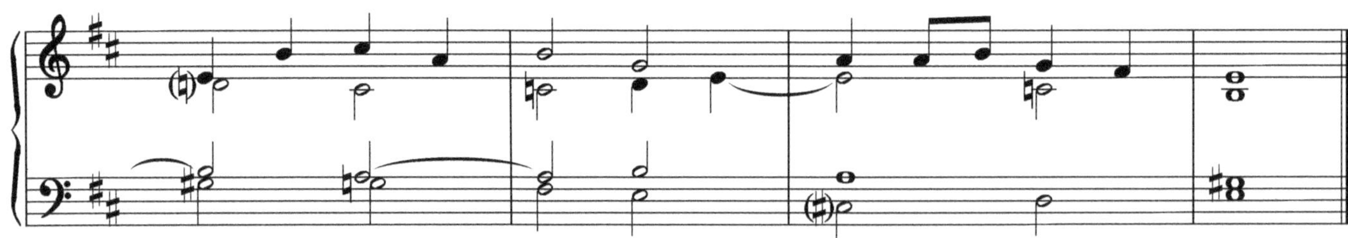